SOUTH AFRICA

Cath Senker

Photographs by Peter Bennett

CHERRYTREE BOOKS

Distributed in the United States by
Cherrytree Books
1980 Lookout Drive
North Mankato, MN 56001

Library of Congress Cataloging-in-Publication Data applied
for.

First Edition
9 8 7 6 5 4 3 2 1

First published in 2005 by
Evans Brothers Ltd
2A Portman Mansions
Chiltern Street
London W1U 6NR

Conceived and produced by

Nutshell
MEDIA

www.nutshellmedialtd.co.uk

Editor: Polly Goodman
Design: Mayer Media Ltd
Cartography: Encompass Graphics Ltd
Artwork: Mayer Media Ltd
Consultants: Jeff Stanfield and Anne Spiring

All photographs were taken by Peter Bennett, except page
28, which is by Orde Eliason/Link Picture Library.
Printed in China.

Acknowledgments
The photographer would like to thank the Anele family,
and the staff and students of Dr. B.W. Vilakazi J.P. School,
KwaMashu, South Africa for all their help with this book.

Cover: Zama and her friends, from left to right: Hlehlehle,
Kinar, Thoko, Zama, and Zinhle.
Title page: Zama plays jump rope with her neighbors in
the street.
This page: A view over the city of Cape Town, with Table
Mountain in the distance.
Contents page: Zama at the new public swimming pool
in KwaMashu.
Glossary page: Majorettes blow whistles as they twirl their
batons during a parade.
Further Information page: Zama's Zulu dance group.
Index: These girls are training to become Sangoma
faith healers.

Contents

My Country

Tuesday, May 3

F1215 Magwaza Road
KwaMashu 8642
KwaZulu-Natal
South Africa

Dear Lee,

Sawubona! (You say "sa-woo-bo-na". This means "hello" in Zulu, my language.)

My name is Zama Anele. I'm 8 years old. I live in a place called KwaMashu, near the city of Durban, in South Africa. I live with my mom, Thandizwe, and my dad, Sipho. My big sister Nonduduzo is 20. She lives in Durban.

I'm learning English, so it's great to have a pen pal to help me practice. I can tell you all about life in South Africa.

Write back soon!

From
Zama

Here's me at home with my mom and dad.

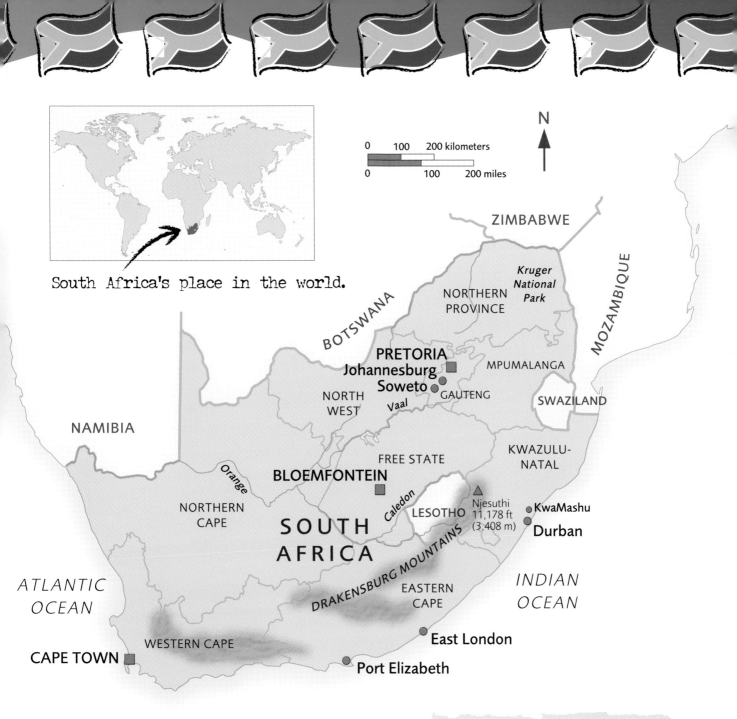

South Africa's place in the world.

Most people in South Africa are black Africans, but there are also white and Asian people. Black and Asian people have only had the same rights as white people since 1994. Most black people are still much poorer than white people.

South Africa is on the southern tip of the African continent, between the Atlantic Ocean and the Indian Ocean.

KwaMashu is a township about 9 miles (15 km) from the city of Durban. Townships are towns on the edge of South African cities.

The government set up KwaMashu in the 1950s as a place for black people to live. At that time, black people had to live in different areas from white people. In 1994, under the new government, KwaMashu became part of Durban.

About half a million people live in the KwaMashu area. Refugees from other African countries come to live there. The population gets bigger every year.

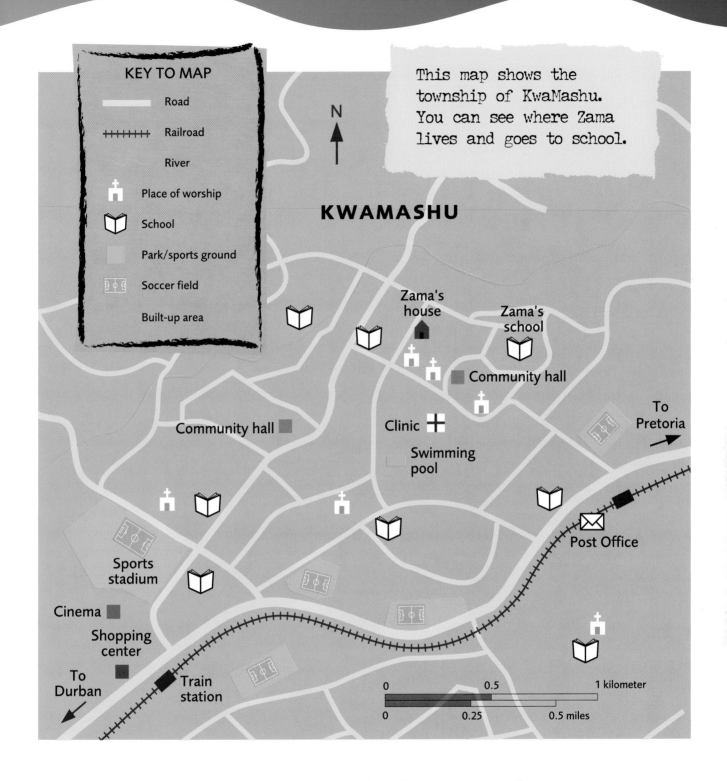

KEY TO MAP

――――	Road
+++++++	Railroad
	River
♦	Place of worship
📖	School
▪	Park/sports ground
⚽	Soccer field
	Built-up area

This map shows the township of KwaMashu. You can see where Zama lives and goes to school.

KWAMASHU

N

Zama's house

Zama's school

Community hall

Community hall

Clinic

Swimming pool

To Pretoria

Post Office

Sports stadium

Cinema

Shopping center

To Durban

Train station

| 0 | 0.5 | 1 kilometer |
| 0 | 0.25 | 0.5 miles |

Some families in KwaMashu live in brick houses with up to four rooms. Most other people live in small huts built close together. Although there is an electricity supply to most houses, many people cannot afford to use it.

Landscape and Weather

The center of South Africa is a high, flat plateau, called the veld. The Drakensburg Mountains in the east are the highest and wettest parts of the country. In the west, where it is lower, there is very little rain and there are often droughts.

South Africa has many wild animals such as lions, elephants, leopards, and rhinos. These white rhinos live in KwaZulu-Natal.

South Africa is south of the Equator, so winter is from June to August and summer is between December and February. Most of the country has warm, sunny days all year round, although winter nights can be very cold in the veld.

The Drakensburg Mountains separate the veld from the lower land on the coast.

KwaMashu's Climate

January

Temperature
75 °F
(24 °C)

Rainfall
5.5 in
(134 mm)

July

Temperature
64 °F
(18 °C)

Rainfall
1.5 in
(39 mm)

At Home

Like most houses in KwaMashu, Zama's house is on one floor. The walls are made from concrete blocks and it has a corrugated iron roof.

Inside there are four rooms: a living room, two bedrooms, and a kitchen. The small kitchen has a gas oven and refrigerator. The toilet is outside.

Zama is playing a clapping game in her front garden with her neighbor Sbongile.

Zama used to share a bedroom with her sister, but after Nonduduzo left home, Zama had the bedroom to herself.

Zama's home has electricity but no water indoors. Water comes from a faucet in the back yard. Many homes in the township do not have running water.

Zama collects water from the faucet outside. The family shares the faucet with their neighbors.

Zama's family doesn't
have a washing machine.
They do all the washing
by hand and hang it out
to dry in the garden.

Zama's family has a
mailbox on the street
outside. Mail is
delivered every
weekday in KwaMashu.
To send her letters,
Zama has to walk to the
post office, just over half
a mile (1 km) away.

Zama checks to see
if there is a letter
from her pen pal.

Saturday, May 28

F1215 Magwaza Road
KwaMashu 8642
KwaZulu-Natal
South Africa

Hi Lee!!

Ninjani? (That's Zulu for "how are you?").

Thanks for your letter. It took two weeks to get here.

After school yesterday I looked after our neighbor's baby for a few hours. I often help my neighbor because she helps mom and dad by looking after me. People around here have always helped each other out. Do you help your neighbors, too?

Write again soon!

From
Zama

↗

Here I am singing the "Click Song" to my neighbor's baby. This is a Zulu song from long ago.

Food and Mealtimes

Zama has some bread and butter for breakfast.

For breakfast, Zama usually has a slice of bread and butter with some water. Her parents drink tea. For lunch, the school meal is always rice and beans.

In South Africa there are lots of street stalls. Zama and her mom often buy bread and vegetables at this one. Food is passed out through the hole in the wire mesh.

For dinner, Zama and her parents usually have canned fish with rice and vegetables. Meat is expensive, so they have chicken for supper just once a week. On Saturday they eat only cold food because it is the Sabbath, which means their holy day. They do not cook on the Sabbath.

Zama and her parents are having canned fish and rice for supper.

Zama and her mom buy canned food and household goods at the local supermarket.

Zama and her mom buy meat from the butcher's and cook it on a stove outside. Using the butcher's stove saves them using their own fuel back home.

Zulu people have always eaten meals that are made mostly from vegetables. Meat is eaten on special occasions. A traditional dish is corn porridge. Sweet potatoes and yams are popular, and so are vegetables such as cabbages and onions. These vegetables grow easily in South Africa.

Sunday, June 19

F1215 Magwaza Road
KwaMashu 8642
KwaZulu-Natal
South Africa

Dear Lee,

You asked me for a traditional Zulu recipe. Here's how to make one of my favorite dishes: spinach with coconut and peanuts.

You will need: 1 lb (500 g) spinach, 1 cup of canned coconut milk, $1/2$ cup of crushed roasted peanuts, 1 chopped onion, 2 teaspoons of chilli sauce, 1 tablespoon of vegetable oil, salt to taste.
Note: Leave out the peanuts if you are allergic to nuts.

1. Wash the spinach thoroughly in salted water.
2. Chop the spinach very finely and drain it.
3. Fry the onion in vegetable oil until it is soft.
4. Add the spinach and cook for 3–5 minutes.
5. Add the other ingredients and cook for another 10–15 minutes.
6. Serve hot with rice.

Sizobonana! (So long!)

Zama

Here's the finished dish, ready to eat!

School Day

Every school day, Zama leaves home at 8:15 a.m. It takes 10 minutes to walk to school, which is a quarter of a mile away.

Children in South Africa start school when they are 5 or 6 years old and move to secondary school when they are 12. Zama's parents have to pay for Zama to go to school. It is only free for the very poorest children in South Africa.

Like most of her friends, Zama walks to school. Most families in KwaMashu don't own cars.

One day a week, the children at Zama's school can wear their own clothes instead of the school uniform.

There are about 240 children in Zama's school. Every morning they say prayers in assembly.

School begins at 8:30 a.m with assembly. Lessons start at 9 a.m and finish at 2 p.m. Zama's main subjects are Zulu, math, and English. She also learns technology, science, history, handwriting, and art.

Each new school year begins in January. The winter vacation lasts from late July until late September. The summer vacation is over Christmas, from early December to late January.

Zama's teacher writes work on the board and asks the children questions.

In South Africa most classes have more than 60 children each. Zama's teacher works with the whole class as a group. Zama may borrow books from the small school library, but there are no computers. Her parents have to pay for her textbooks.

Zama and her schoolfriends tidy up the litter in the playground. They are learning how to look after the environment.

Tuesday, July 19

F1215 Magwaza Road
KwaMashu 8642
KwaZulu-Natal
South Africa

Sawubona Lee!

I'm glad you enjoyed the spinach dish.

Today was my favorite day at school because we had dance practice. I'm in a Zulu dance group and my school won the School Zulu Dancing Championships last year. We're hoping to win again this year. Our dances are all about Zulu history and praising our kings of the past.

What's your favorite subject at school? Write back soon and tell me.

From

Zama

Here I am with my dance group, holding a Zulu drum. The drum is Africa's oldest musical instrument.

Off to Work

Zama's dad works as a bricklayer. There is a lot of building work in South Africa. The government has begun a big project to repair roads, schools, and houses, especially in the townships. Downtown KwaMashu is going to be rebuilt and there will be a new hospital in the area.

Zama's dad at work building a wall. Like many people in KwaMashu, he is a casual worker, taking jobs when he can.

A sugarcane worker harvesting cane. Sugarcane is a major crop in the area around Durban.

Many people in KwaMashu work in factories that make clothes or food. Others have jobs in tourism. They serve tourists in Durban, who surf on the beaches there. Some people look after tourists who visit the townships.

These new trucks at Durban harbor are about to be loaded on to a ship and sold abroad. Durban has a huge port, which is important for South Africa's trade.

Free Time

After school and on weekends, Zama likes playing with her friends who live nearby. Their favorite game is jump rope, but they make other games from things they find. They love rolling old car tires around the street.

Soccer is South Africa's favorite sport. Many people live a long way from a sports field but it's easy to play soccer in the street.

Majorettes accompany Zulu bands during parades, twirling their batons. They are an important part of Zulu culture.

Monday, August 8

F1215 Magwaza Road
KwaMashu 8642
KwaZulu-Natal
South Africa

Hi Lee,

It's the school winter vacation at the moment but the days are still sunny and warm. Last week mom took me swimming at the new pool in KwaMashu. It was only built last year and it's huge! Before that, the nearest swimming pool was in Durban, but now there are lots of new things being built here. I hope it will make our lives much better.

From

Zama

Here I am at the brand new swimming pool. I can't swim yet, but I love splashing in the water.

Religion

Most South Africans are Christians. There are thousands of different Churches (Christian groups). Each one has different forms of worship. One of the biggest is the Zion Independent Church. It does not allow drinking alcohol, eating pork, or smoking.

Zama's family belongs to the Pentecostal Church. Members of this Church hold services outdoors, under trees or by streams.

Zama, her sister, and mom, ready for church on Sunday. Zama and her sister are wearing religious dress.

Many black South Africans follow traditional religions, such as faith healing and animism. Faith healers treat their patients' minds as well as their bodies. Animists believe that natural objects such as stones and trees have souls.

This Zionist priest, from the Zion Christian Church, is blessing a girl.

These women are Sangoma faith healers. They are wearing traditional dress and have their medicines laid out on the table in front.

Fact File

Capital City: Pretoria. Cape Town (above) and Bloemfontein are also capital cities.

Other Major Cities: Durban, Johannesburg, Soweto, Port Elizabeth.

Size: 468,934 square miles (1,219,912 km^2).

Population: About 42.7 million people live in South Africa.

Languages: There are 11 official languages in South Africa: Afrikaans, English, Ndebele, Pedi, Sotho, Swazi, Tsonga, Tswana, Venda, Xhosa, and Zulu.

Flag: The red, white, and blue come from the Dutch and British flags. The black, green, and gold come from the flags of the African freedom movements. The "Y" shape shows that all the peoples will go forward together.

Motto: "Diverse peoples unite." This means that all the different peoples of South Africa — black, Asian, mixed-race, and white — should work together.

Main Religions: 68 percent of South Africans are Christians and 29 percent follow traditional African religions. The rest are Muslims and Hindus.

Main Industries: Mining, auto assembly, metalworking, machinery, textiles, iron and steel, chemicals, food products.

Currency: The rand. There are 100 cents in a South African rand.

Longest River: The Orange River is about 1,300 miles (2,100 km) long.

Wildlife: South Africa has 20 national parks where people can see wildlife including elephants, rhinoceroses, buffalo, lions, leopards, cheetahs, giraffes, and many kinds of reptiles and birds.

Highest Mountain: The highest mountain range is the Drakensburg Mountains. The highest point is at Njesuthi, 11,178 ft (3,408 m).

Famous People: Nelson Mandela, born in 1918, was sent to prison in 1962 for fighting for African freedom. Freed in 1990, he became the first black South African president in 1994. Desmond Tutu (born 1931) has spent his life working for equal rights for all people in South Africa, and received a Nobel Peace Prize in 1984. Singer and human rights campaigner Miriam Makeba, born in 1932, was exiled from 1960 to 1990 but continued to campaign around the world.

Stamps: South African stamps show wildlife, important buildings, sports, people, and events from history.

Glossary

corn A plant that is eaten as a vegetable or used to make flour.

drought A long period of time when there is little or no rain.

Equator An imaginary line around the middle of the Earth.

faith healing Using the power of belief and prayer to heal sick people.

harbor An area of water on the coast where ships can shelter.

majorettes Girls who walk along with a marching band, spinning, throwing, and catching a long stick called a baton.

national parks and reserves Areas of land where the wildlife and plants are protected but people are allowed to visit.

plateau An area of flat land that is higher than the land around it.

refugees People who have to leave their country because of war or because their views or religious beliefs make it dangerous to stay.

running water Water that is brought into a building in pipes and can be used from faucets.

Sabbath A religious day of rest.

Sangoma African healers who are believed to have special spiritual powers.

sugarcane A tall plant with thick stems, that is used to make sugar.

tourism The business of providing services to vacationers.

township A town on the edge of a South African city.

traditional Something that has been done for a long time.

veld A high plateau region in the centre of South Africa.

Zulu One of the black peoples of South Africa. Zama's family is Zulu.

Further Information

Information books:

Brownlie, Alison. *We Come from South Africa*. Chicago: Raintree, 2000.

Cornell, Christine. *Zulu of Southern Africa*. New York: Power Kids Press, 1997.

Gogerly, Liz. *The Freeing of Nelson Mandela*. Chicago: Raintree, 2004.

Raatma, Lucia. *South Africa*. Minneapolis, MN: Compass Books, 2001.

Tames, Richard. *Turning Points in History: The End of Apartheid*. Chicago: Heinemann Library, 2000.

Fiction:

Batezat Sisulu, Elinor. *The Day Gogo Went to Vote*. Megan Tingley Books, 1999.

Daly, Niki. *Where's Jamela?*. Farrar Straus Giroux, 2004.

Morris, Tony and Tonge, Neil. *Freedom Song, the Story of Nelson Mandela*. Hodder Wayland, 2002.

Web sites:

CIA Factbook
www.cia.gov/cia/publications/factbook/
Basic facts and figures about South Africa and other countries.

South Africa Tourism Website
http://www.southafrica.net/
Information about travel to South Africa.

Durban City Website
http://www.durban.gov.za/eThekwini
Information about Durban and its townships.

KwaMashu Township Tourism
http://www.kzn.org.za/kzn/778.xml
Information about KwaMashu.

Index